W9-AJT-575

11/07

I Think That It Is Wonderful

By David Korr
Illustrated by A. Delaney

Featuring Jim Henson's Sesame Street Muppets

This educational book was created in cooperation with the Children's Television Workshop, producers of Sesame Street. Children do not have to watch the television show to benefit from this book. Workshop revenues from this product will be used to help support CTW educational projects.

A Sesame Street / Golden Press Book

Published by Western Publishing Company, Inc. in conjunction with Children's Television Workshop.

A B C D E F G H I J

I Think That It Is Wonderful

I think that it is wonderful
to wake up with the sun
when it has just begun
to shine.
Hello, bright morning sun.

I think that it is wonderful
to hear the waking street
as all those busy feet
go by.
Hello, Sesame Street.

Me think that it is wonderful
to wake up wanting food.
To be in hungry mood
is swell.
(Don't worry, my tummy stop growling
after me have breakfast.)
Hello, food food food food!

I think that it is wonderful
to stretch from head to heels.
When I get up it feels
just right.
Hello, knees, toes, and heels.

I think that it is wonderful
to scrub each part of me
to make sure I will be
all clean.
Hello, clean, spiffy me.

The Strangest Word

A friend of mine once used a word,
The sound of which is so absurd
I was amazed at what I'd heard
And stood there, quite astounded.

I finally gasped, "Is that word *real*?"
My friend said, "Yes, and what you feel
Is just the thing to help reveal
This strange absurd word's meaning!"

My mouth went wide; so did my eyes.
In fact, they grew to twice their size
As I stood there in shocked surprise.
I don't know how I lasted.
For what I felt was what I'd learned
Is meant by—*flabbergasted*!

When My Imagination

When my imagination
Takes me by the mind,
It leads me off so far, so fast,
My body's left behind.
Yet that's when I am *most* myself,
Lost in wish and dream,
And coming back, I smile and think,
"I'm more than I might seem."

8801168

A Silly Mystery

Here's a pretty mystery
without a clue that I can see.
If you are you and I am I
and together we are we,
of course it then makes sense to say
that they are he and she.
But if you and I and he and she
are all in one big bunch,
then where are they and who are we
and is it time for lunch?

HOOPER'S STORE

What Is a Song?

What is a song?

What *is* that magical ribbon of sound
that swirls and twines 'round you and me,
weaving words and music
in proper one

two

three?

What makes a song?

What *is* it makes us sing along,
our voices joining up and down
with sounds that roll and sway and beat,
our feet and fingers tapping
in proper one

two

three?

What *is* a song?

Oh, I Was So Embarrassed!

Have you ever been embarrassed?

Have you ever felt so foolish
You just wished to run away?
"Why, yes!" you cry? Then hear how I
Embarrassed ME today.

I took the bus all by myself,
In my little coat and cap.
I felt so proud, until I sat
On someone else's lap!

"Oh, no!" I said. "What have I done?
Would you excuse me, please?
I should have looked before I sat
And landed on your knees!"

The woman on whose lap I perched
Was, oh, so very kind.
She told me that she understood,
She really did not mind.

I said, "Oh, thank you very much.
You have not frowned a bit.
You understand I did not mean
To make you undersit!"

With that I stood up hurriedly
And found another place.
Embarrassment most certainly
Was painted on my face.

Since you have felt embarrassed, too,
I do not have to say
How glad I am that I found out
The feeling goes away!

There Is a Road

There is a road
I call my own.
It beckons me
when I'm alone,
this special road
that seems to be
a road I planned
so perfectly
it winds and bends
at my command
and takes me where
I wish to be—
atop a hill,
beneath a tall old tree.

There Is a Place

There is a place
that's mine alone,
where I'll go still
when I am grown.
A long road ends
atop a hill,
beneath a tree,
and there I fill
my mind with thoughts
of what might be,
and watch the leaves
sway over me
like waves on some
green, gentle sea.

I've Been Wondering

I've been wondering.
I've been wondering about all kinds of things.
Big things, like buildings and boulevards.
Little things, like lima beans, and locks,
And the label on my favorite overalls.
I've been wondering about in-between things, too—
Mailboxes, and my bathtub, and benches in the park.
What I wonder is: are they still *there*
When I'm in bed, and all I see's the dark?

When You're New on the Street

When you're new on the street
and the people you meet
you've never met before.

When the neighborhood's strange
and you're confused by the change
that waits outside your door,

What you need is just time
and to tell yourself, "I'm
still learning my way around."

Everybody you greet
was once new on the street.
We've *all* felt lost before.

A new home can feel strange,
but that feeling will change
and you'll find, more and more,

That what you need is just time
and to tell yourself, "I'm
still learning my way around."

The Mirror Poem

No mirror's big enough for Snuff
   to see all Snuff at once.
He could try doing it in bits,
   but that would take him months.
So I walk all around him
   and tell him what I see.
And then, because he is my friend,
   he does the same for me.

So Many Things

So many things,
So many, many things to do,
Too many for one day,
Too many for my little feet
To take me all that way;
Too many for my little hands,
My little eyes and ears;
But tomorrow I will start again.
I'm afraid this may take years.

I Think That It Is Wonderful

I think that it is wonderful
that I can see a star,
when it's so very far
away.
Good night, faraway star.

I think that it is wonderful
that I can hear birds sing,
when outside everything
is still.
Good night, bird on the wing.

Me think that it is wonderful
to eat my food all up,
especially at sup-
per time.
(Or lunch time or breakfast time.
It not matter.)
Night, night, delicious food.

I think that it is wonderful
that I can smell a rose.
I'm so glad that my nose
knows how.
Good night, sweet-smelling rose.

I think that it is wonderful
to hug my Teddy bear.
It doesn't matter where
we are.
Sleep tight, Teddy, my bear.

Good night, faraway star.
Good night, bird on the wing.
Good night, delicious food.
Good night, sweet-smelling rose.
Good night, Teddy, my bear.

Good night, good night, good night.